The CEO Game Changer Testimonials

In this increasingly changing and complex business, social and political environment, individuals and organisations need to obtain not just information, but critical and selective information, which is accurate, timely, and relevant. Over the last 40 years, I have been involved with business at every level and have read widely. Anthony Moss's book, *The CEO Game Changer* contains a multitude of recipes required to achieve business success. Congratulations, Anthony!

This book is full of incredible wisdom, combined with an easy and logical roadmap that can be implemented to bring about success for the business, the CEO and other critical stakeholders.

The book is well structured and includes relevant case studies demonstrating the theory. Anthony Moss has skilfully applied his knowledge and intellect, built-up through working with hundreds of businesses over his working life; the content is supported by questionnaires, CEO and director interviews, which synthesise Anthony's contemporary leadership and relevant knowledge. This is what I love about Anthony's book. It deals with the tomorrow's rather than the yesterdays to help people build their future.

"This is one of the best reads, I have undertaken in my own personal and business journey; congratulations!"

There are many, excellent moments in reading *The CEO Game Changer*. I have selected a wonderful reflection on page 97 of his book. Anthony identifies as an outcome of his work, 'energised leadership focused on measuring and managing the right things'; this in my humble opinion, encapsulates the quality of Anthony's insight, and the contribution that *The CEO Game Changer* will make to any CEO who wants to build a better business.

DR JIM TAGGART, OAM

In this increasingly specialist world, we seldom learn to manage business. This is a challenge for any CEO/MD—the business journey is full of highs and lows, pitfalls and backward steps. At SFA, operating with an Advisory Board for the past several years has given insight, strategic direction and growth both nationally and internationally. The Advisory Board has helped navigate that wild ride and produce extraordinary results. This book is a must-read for all those in business seeking success.

BILL MORRISON, Managing Director, Street Furniture Australia

The CEO Game Changer is packed with wisdom, case studies and exercises that will help any CEO to establish a powerful Advisory Board. In turn, the Advisory Board can help you elevate the capability and unlock the potential of you and your senior leaders. A must read.

ROB PYNE, Founder, Realizer

A true game changer that highlights how strategic insights of an Advisory Board can unlock productivity, profitability, and growth. A transformative guide for founders and CEOs seeking expert perspectives to propel their organisations with insightful tips only someone who has walked the talk will know.

ISHAN GALAPATHY, Operational Excellence Strategist, Author and Speaker

Every CEO needs perspective. This book explores how an Advisory Board can help CEOs maintain that perspective; a must read.

PETER ROSSDALE, Managing Director, Rossdale Pty Ltd

As a CEO, the establishment of our Advisory Board has been pivotal to our success. Their diverse expertise and objective insights enhance our decision-making and strategic planning. Our Advisory Board's invaluable feedback helps us navigate challenges and seize new opportunities, while their networks open doors to partnerships that fuel our growth.

BLAIR SADDINGTON, General Manager, Street Furniture Australia

The concept of an Advisory Board is something that could truly be a game-changer for CEOs, and reading this book is an invaluable resource for all CEOs exploring this idea.

ANDREA MCDONALD, CEO | Director, Barker Ryan Stewart

As a futurist I've learnt that the path to business success is rarely a straight line. So how do you know where to start? As Anthony brilliantly highlights, it's not about where to start—it's about astutely travelling alongside others. Making the game-changing shift from tunnel vision to seeing the big picture, with a far more dynamic range of inspiring possibilities.

DAVE WILD, Futurist

As a self-taught business owner of forty-one years, I draw success from surrounding myself with people who are smarter than me, especially where I know my skills are limited. Being a part of a structured CEO group provides me a safe place to discuss my wins and failures with like-minded business owners and CEOs who all strive to do and be better.

A well-run group provides you with both encouragement and accountability in a respectful environment, irrespective of your abilities. It also provides you with shared experiences where you can draw knowledge and inspiration.

One of my favourite analogies of our CEO group is that business (and life) is like a game of *Snakes and Ladders*, Business is never a smooth ride, it's full of big ups and big downs, especially as we all experienced the volatile changes during a period of pre and post COVID. Many of us drew on the combined wisdom of our group as we navigated the various effects of change.

Owning and running a business doesn't have to be commercially lonely; you can navigate the journey to achieve your goals and assist others to achieve theirs by being a part of a business group. I can't recommend it highly enough.

Anthony's book spells out in detail the advantages of surrounding yourself with your 'A Team' of supporters vested in your success and he explains how to do it. It's a great read!

JOHN GRIMA, Managing Director, Kellyville Pets

I've run my own businesses for the last 20 years, and through my first and biggest business venture—that I eventually sold—I wish I knew having a board of advisors was something that could really assist. Self-funded in those days and manically busy, I didn't have time for family, let alone finding mentors or taking time to get a board of advisors together. Where would I have started?! Running day-to-day and wearing all the stress that comes at you is a hard gig. If I could go back and give myself a gift that would have helped, I would have called Anthony. An amazing leader who has wisdom, foresight and an innovative mindset. I really could have done with his influence.

Just to have had someone in my corner that already knew about the many and varied struggles I encountered would have made the road a smoother one. I'm lucky to have met you now, Anthony. Being a serial founder, future me is going to be even luckier!

Thank you for your support and friendship—I'm grateful I found you. To anyone in a similar position—read the book! It's a wonderful way to get the edge that all business leaders need.

JODIE MOULE, Co-Founder, behavjōr

The role of the Advisory Board played a crucial element in the growth, development, and ultimate success of my business, Craig & Rhodes Pty Ltd.

The CEO Game Changer by Anthony Moss provides business owners with a clear strategy and process of how and why to set up an Advisory Board that will take any business to the next level.

Be prepared to be challenged by the process of inviting independent, smart and commercial people into your business, but also be prepared to celebrate the step change in your business performance both internally and to your clients when the positive results and financial returns are measured.

The CEO Game Changer is just that. It is recommended reading for all CEOs who want success.

ANDREW HALMARICK, CEO, Craig & Rhodes

THE CEO
GAME
CHANGER

THE CEO GAME CHANGER

HOW AN ADVISORY BOARD CAN UNLEASH YOUR BUSINESS POTENTIAL

ANTHONY MOSS

GRAMMAR
FACTORY
— EST. 2013 —

Grammar Factory Publishing
MacMillan Company Limited
25 Telegram Mews, 39th Floor, Suite 3906
Toronto, Ontario, Canada
M5V 3Z1

www.grammarfactory.com

Moss, Anthony
The CEO Game Changer: How an Advisory Board Can Unleash Your
Business Potential

Paperback ISBN 978-1-989737-95-8
eBook ISBN 978-1-989737-96-5

1. BUS025000 BUSINESS & ECONOMICS / Entrepreneurship.
2. BUS071000 BUSINESS & ECONOMICS / Leadership.|
3. BUS041000 BUSINESS & ECONOMICS / Management.

PRODUCTION CREDITS
Cover design by Designerbility
Interior layout design by Setareh Ashrafologhalai
Book production and editorial services by Grammar Factory Publishing

GRAMMAR FACTORY'S CARBON NEUTRAL
PUBLISHING COMMITMENT
Grammar Factory Publishing is proud to be neutralising the carbon
footprint of all printed copies of its authors' books printed by or ordered
directly through Grammar Factory or its affiliated companies through the
purchase of Gold Standard-Certified International Offsets.

To Denise, Elizabeth and James.
You are the light in my world.

Contents

PART TWO
THE GAME CHANGER

Chapter 3
How Does an Advisory Board Work?

Chapter 4
Building Your Advisory Board

Conclusion

Acknowledgements

Disclaimer

NONE OF THIS is legal advice, considered legal practice, or current. The information in this book is my opinion, based on my over thirty years of commercial experience. As laws may change post-publication of this book, the reader is responsible for engaging their legal resource when considering an Advisory Board. The terms of the Advisory Board, the process of appointment and termination of members, should be reviewed with your legal representative, as should the operating nature of the Advisory Board, how decisions are made post meetings and tracked. An Advisory Board is designed to be an arms-length advisory body with no decision-making authority, undue influence, or obligation to the company or CEO other than to participate in meetings. All care must be taken to ensure that the independence of an Advisory Board is not compromised in a way that the board could be deemed to be acting as shadow directors.

Foreword

IT'S 3:00 AM, and my mind is awake with the noise of work: challenges, ideas and business opportunities all going around in my drowsy head. I pick up my phone to jot down the four things circling my brain and try to get back to sleep.

I have been running my business for over twenty years. Although I have learned to live with the ups and downs of being in business, the challenges of being the CEO have been pretty consistent. There's always a new question to answer or a problem to solve. How do I create an inspiring yet executable strategy? When should I put on more sales resources? Do I need a more experienced finance team? Is running without profit okay while I grow this area of the business? Is this new product a good idea? Should we just open our own office in the UK?

Experience has taught me that, many times, the answers lie within you, thanks to my many hours of thinking at 3:00 am. What's also true is that extracting those answers is almost impossible to do alone.

In 2005, I was trying to run two businesses, an industrial design business and a construction product sales business, which were both underperforming. It was clear I was failing.

My father suggested I ring a guy named Ross for help; he used to sell capital equipment and could give me some sage advice on how to move forward, but I didn't. The product business carried on for another year. I opened a warehouse and employed a GM and several salespeople; we imported a heap of products no one wanted, and I had no choice but to shrink the business to a single salesperson and figure out plan B. At this point, I rang Ross and asked, 'Can you help advise me on running this business?' Ross agreed, and we had our first Advisory Board member. I also asked my father for help. When he agreed, that was it, the Advisory Board was in place.

As luck would have it, Paul, the salesman I kept on, was a genius and managed to sell all our stock so we could restart the journey of growing a construction product business. We have adjusted the Advisory Board to suit the business's needs along the journey. In 2012, Anthony Moss joined the Advisory Board and soon became an Advisory Chair.

Since 2012, we have renamed and rebranded the business into Makinex, set up offices in the USA, set up and closed down offices in the UK, invented several award-winning products, created a renewables product business, had several years of various profits and a few years of losses. Paul and I headed up the business for many of these years and have relied heavily on the sound, objective, higher-level advice of the Advisory Board. There have also been times when we came in with too much gusto but not enough open-mindedness. At these times, when we didn't listen to the advice of the board, we later realised our failings.

Today, I am fortunate to have a motivated and qualified leadership team to work with, along with the whole Makinex team. These are the people who make so many strategic day-to-day decisions for the company. Still, as we come up against larger opportunities and obstacles, I look forward to bringing them to our next board meeting to ensure we can leverage the board's knowledge and strategic thinking.

The Advisory Board has been a key partner in my business journey and should be for yours, too. This book explains how to set up and leverage your own Advisory Board, which I would recommend to any Founder or CEO.

Anthony, thank you for all your support over the past twelve years; I look forward to unpacking a few more challenges with you and the board in our next meeting and all our meetings to come.

RORY KENNARD
Founder and CEO, Makinex
www.makinex.com.au

Introduction

BUILDING AND RUNNING businesses has always been my passion. In the late 1980s, Daler-Rowney, a 200-year-old, then family-owned company, gave me a great opportunity to set up a new business in the US. I moved from the UK with a suitcase of samples and a bucket load of youthful ambition.

Tasked with building the new business, I developed distribution models, hired a sales team, sourced suppliers, directed marketers and created new products. We acquired and integrated two other businesses, including an offshore manufacturer, and successfully sold products to some of the world's biggest retailers, including Walmart, Macy's and Saks Fifth Avenue. We exported around the globe.

It was stressful and challenging at times but also exhilarating and fun; I was fortunate to be invited to sit alongside the owners and other senior executives on the board of directors.

This experience of creating a thriving business—an enterprise that generated wealth, employed staff who developed new skills, and helped drive economic growth and international trade—galvanised my passion for building great businesses.

After ten years in the US and moving to Australia, I had the opportunity to grow two other businesses as CEO before establishing my consulting practice in 2003 and Lead Your Industry in 2012. Since starting my practice, I've worked with over 180 companies, including private companies, family businesses, large corporations, start-ups and associations.

I've helped companies in all kinds of trouble, from looming closure to cutting costs, desperate to find revenue and new markets. Watching these businesses transform from stress and unhappiness to triumph and success brings me great joy. Seeing the amazing impact that thriving businesses can have on communities and society inspired me to write this book. Despite many business success stories, to the CEO and managing director, running a business can sometimes feel like playing a continuous game of Snakes and Ladders.

Remember the game you played as a child when the fate of your dice determined whether you'd scale forward several steps or slide down the snake?

Businesses can experience great weeks, months and years when everything comes together, a new product or service succeeds, sales budgets are easily exceeded, and profit and cash flow are promising. It feels great to be the CEO during these times.

Contrast this with the dark weeks, months, or sometimes years when external (or internal) shocks hit, surprises happen, numbers fall short, previously successful strategies don't work, or a key person leaves. It's not so great to be the CEO on those days when it feels like nothing is working out.

CEOs are always searching for the ladders while avoiding the snakes.

The stats are clear: over sixty per cent of businesses will fail in their first five years.[1] This is a terrible statistic, especially given the trauma a failed business can cause. Ripples of that trauma are felt far and wide by staff, suppliers, customers, shareholders and their families.

Many underperforming businesses can experience the same challenges. They don't fail; they keep going, but they are stuck in a quagmire that I describe as *Fighting for Position*. Businesses in this mode are under constant stress, with erratic performance, insufficient cash, uncertainty and inertia. They are not happy places to work for the people or the CEO.

Then, there are successful businesses that break through the Fighting for Position stage. They transform themselves, and many become industry leaders. They're companies like Makinex Pty Ltd, taking a leading industry position by designing and manufacturing innovative construction and power tools (see www.makinex.com.au); they're Street Furniture Australia, the leading street furniture manufacturer using design and durability to transform places in the public realm (see www.streetfurniture.com) and they're Tiger Tribe, designing portable toys to nurture confidence and creativity in kids (see www.tigertribe.com.au). The recipe for success is relatively simple to identify, however difficult it may be to achieve. A successful business has:

- a great idea (product or service) that is different from its competitors,

- customers who value that idea and are prepared to pay for it,

- a positive culture that attracts great talent,

- the 'Right Strategy' and Business Model,

---

1 https://www.boq.com.au/business/small-business/business-knowledge-hub/opening-a-small-business/the-top-ten-reasons-small-businesses-fail

- a learning mindset (learning from experience, from experts, from the market),

- and, most importantly, a leader who can mould together a group of capable, driven people into a high-performing team.

For even the most experienced CEO, combining all this at the right time while navigating shifting opportunities and threats can feel like rolling the dice.

It is even more challenging in a private company

John Maxwell, a US leadership thinker, is reputed to have said businesses cannot outperform the capability of their leadership. The challenge for most private company leaders is that until a reasonable degree of scale is reached in a small company, its appetite and ambition are always greater than its capability.

The premise of this book is that for the right company, with shareholders and leaders that have an appetite and ambition for growth, an Advisory Board is an ideal model that can fill that gap in capability, enabling the business to grow and evolve. Indeed, the Advisory Board can continue to evolve itself, changing its members to comprise people with the necessary skills and capabilities that the business needs for each next growth stage. An Advisory Board can be applicable in many circumstances; this book focuses on its value to the CEO of a private company.

For this book, here's how I define a private company: it is an organisation with leadership that has a very clear ambition and an appetite to achieve that ambition more swiftly than current resources allow. The existing leadership team may all be great people with the potential to grow, but they need to develop new skills and experience, which takes time.

This may be a business with fifty staff and only a few years into existence, or a larger family business with 250 staff seeking a more dominant position in their industry. Most importantly, the CEOs and leaders of these businesses are willing to be vulnerable, acknowledge their skill gaps, and learn from others who have already trodden the path they seek to take.

In all private companies, the pressure to solve the conundrum of having champagne aspirations with ginger beer resources falls on you, the CEO. How well are you equipped? There is an assumption that being given (or assuming) the title of CEO means you already have all the skills to do the job and be at peak performance all the time. Is that fair, and how often is it true? Surprisingly, you are human; you are a work in progress, great at some things, not so great at others, on fire on some days, perhaps not so hot on others.

Life at the top can be a Commercially Lonely place.

In successful small companies, the CEO needs decision-making confidence, and the leadership team needs the appropriate skills to take the business to the next level. Capability evolves over time. Unless there is an internal or external catalyst for dramatic change, the step-change in capability is likely to be slow and incremental. The same applies to you. If your skills and frame of reference remain the same, your capability also remains the same. Maybe you're already upskilling yourself, your people and your leadership team. From time to time, you engage expert consultants to address known challenges. If you have a board, your discussions might be well-meaning, but perhaps the conversations tend to be repetitive or focus too much on operations and not enough on strategy. You're doing everything possible to scale beyond Fighting for Position, but you know something is missing. The pressure to find the right solution falls squarely on your shoulders.

Commercially Lonely

Sitting at the top of a company is what I describe as a *Commercially Lonely* position. People assume that the title of CEO bestows you with superhuman skills to achieve all tasks no matter what the needs of the company. This expectation comes from the people you lead and your fellow shareholders and directors. There are often decisions that need to be made that cannot be discussed with other people in the organisation, and there is pressure from the board, whether perceived or real, to 'have the answers'. This is how it feels to be Commercially Lonely.

Constructively Discontent

CEOs are also hardwired to think there is a better way, even if they can't quite articulate what 'better' looks like or how to achieve it. Despite their success, they know that the market share could be greater, efficiency could be better, and company profits could be higher. The thought pattern is this: *I love what we're achieving, but we could be doing much more.* This powerful motivator is inherent in most CEOs; it motivates the CEO to drive the next growth stage. However, communicating your discontent can have the opposite effect on your leadership team. Being what I call *Constructively Discontent* can demotivate your team if they consistently perceive you, their CEO, as dissatisfied.

You're playing the business version of Snakes and Ladders, navigating the highs and lows in one minute, with total control, while losing it all the next minute, causing a huge impact. You must find the right balance in setting the performance expectations of your team to motivate, not demotivate. At the same time, you often must take charge in pressing circumstances when it is not appropriate or possible to explore your options before making a decision. This is the role you have chosen. You can choose to stay in this mode, figuring it all out as you go and evolving slowly, or you can fast-track your learning and build a support structure around you that can lend you the skills to take your business to the next stage swiftly and with confidence.

By choosing to pick up this book, I hope that you've chosen the latter. I aim to share the learning I have gained to assist you in transforming your organisations into successful, resilient businesses that build wealth for all stakeholders and contribute to a better society. I contend that for the CEOs and directors of private companies, establishing an Advisory Board can be a game changer in the business growth process. I will share with you the unique benefits of building an Advisory Board, case studies of companies that have benefited from the structure, and how to set up your own Advisory Board. Of course, you'll continue to play the game of Snakes and Ladders, but you'll have renewed confidence. You won't be alone; you'll work with others vested in your success. This book will hopefully be a catalyst, stimulating your thinking about how your journey as CEO may evolve.

What is the CEO Game Changer?

Based on my experience as CEO of four organisations and coach of over 180 businesses since 2003, being a business leader is, in equal measure, both exhilarating and challenging.

It requires skills, drive and resilience. The CEO has a unique impact on a business; indeed, I would go as far as to say that the skills and mindset of the CEO are Key Performance Indicators of an organisation's capability to grow. If the CEO must ensure their skills are developing and their mindset is right for the job, then appointing the right Advisory Board (AB), I argue, *is* the CEO Game Changer. While there is never a guarantee of business success, appointing your AB can increase the odds, fast-track your and your teams' learning, and enable you to make better decisions confidently.

Your Advisory Board is your hand-picked, experienced A-team of supporters who walk alongside you, sharing the challenges and opportunities of building your great business. Separate from a board of directors, an Advisory Board structure applies to many types of organisations. For example, it can complement a Governance Board in a larger or not-for-profit business. However, this book explores the benefits of an Advisory Board specifically for CEOs of private companies.

Of course, even after appointing an Advisory Board, you'll continue playing the commercial Snakes and Ladders game, no matter what business you run. However, appointing an AB will make those slides down the snakes much less frequent and devastating. You won't be alone; you'll be working with others who are vested in your success and can help guide you when you need support.

What you will learn from this book

Every business has its own unique set of problems. As such, each business needs its own arsenal of tools and solutions. The fact that you are reading this book means that the idea of an Advisory Board for your business intrigues you. In this book, you will find out the pros and cons of an AB, how relatively easy it is to set up, what to expect, what a good one looks like, and what you will need to do as CEO to make it work.

In Part One: The Challenge, we examine the business challenges you may face as a company *Fighting for Position* in your industry. Chapter 1 explores the potential issues holding your business back and the benefits an Advisory Board can bring. Chapter 2 is about identifying when you're ready for change and understanding the different stages of business development.

In Part Two: The Game Changer, we explore the workings of an Advisory Board. Chapter 3 explains what an Advisory Board is and how it should perform for your business. You will also learn about some other useful CEO advisory alternatives. Chapter 4 identifies whether an Advisory Board is right for you and then discusses how to build one. You'll learn how to structure meetings, find members, and measure your success, among other useful topics.

In short, by the end of this book, you'll be able to decide if establishing an Advisory Board is the right step for you and your business and, if so, how to go about it.

PART ONE

THE
CHALLENGE

1

Breaking out of Fighting for Position

*We have proved that our business has
tremendous potential if we can add
the right skills and resources.*

LEAVING THE OFFICE that evening, Ben forced a smile, but beneath the surface, a knot of worry tightened in his gut. Sure, he'd overcome challenges before, but this felt different. The market was getting saturated, competition fiercer. Being a reliable supplier was no longer enough. He craved to be a leader, a brand that customers actively sought out, not just another name on a long list of vendors.

Demanding high-profile clients and competitor copies were mere symptoms of a larger problem. Bolt & Co. needed to evolve and carve out a unique space in the market. But the path forward was shrouded in uncertainty. Invest in aggressive marketing; double down on R&D for even more groundbreaking products; partner with a larger company, potentially sacrificing some control. Every option came with its own set of risks.

He remembered the thrill of starting from scratch in the early days. Now, the weight of responsibility for a growing company, for the livelihoods of his team, felt heavy. He yearned for a crystal ball, a glimpse into the future that would show him the right course of action. But there was no such thing. The road ahead was foggy, and Ben knew it was up to him to navigate it. The highs of being a CEO were undeniable, but so were the lows of uncertainty. The future might be uncertain, but one thing was clear: he wouldn't let Bolt & Co. stagnate. He would lead them forward even if the path remained unclear.

This is a typical scenario for the CEO of a private company in Fighting for Position mode. Most decisions in business are rarely black and white, zero-sum, based on perfect knowledge. In short, you can't predict with 100% accuracy how your customers, your people, or the competition will respond to a decision. You decide with a perspective on the outcome you want. That perspective is formed on the best available information and your intuition about the likely outcome or outcomes. Your perspective is key. How is that perspective influenced?

In an ideal world, your perspective (and decisions) are formed after assessment of the information available and time for reflection on the risks.

The reality in business is rarely close to this ideal; decisions are often made quickly, with imperfect or no information and in an environment of stress, whether it is cash flow constraints, challenges with customers, suppliers, regulators, your people, and more.

In this cauldron of stress, it is easy for the CEO to convince themselves that they are pretty good at decision-making. And yet, there are also times when quick decisions don't pan out.

So, if CEO decision-making is based on probability rather than reliable information, how can the CEO increase their odds of getting it right?

Jeff Bezos, the founder of Amazon, has succinctly articulated the challenge of CEO decision-making. He talks about Type 1 and Type 2 Decisions. Type 1 Decisions are big, consequential decisions that are likely to be irreversible. Type 2 Decisions are relatively easy to reverse and can, therefore, be made quickly in the cauldron of stress.[2]

He suggests that Type 1 Decisions should be made 'Methodically, carefully, slowly, with great deliberation and consultation.'

For many CEOs, depending on what stage your business is in, making decisions methodically, slowly, with great deliberation and with the right consultation is a challenge.

At what stage is your business?

The challenge for you as CEO is to drive the organisation to break through to the next growth stage. At each stage, the focus, leadership style and skills required differ.

CEOs must address the commercial challenges of building the right team, leading the right culture, and successfully penetrating their target market profitably as they move through the Fighting for Position stage.

2   https://www.sec.gov/Archives/edgar/data/1018724/000119312516530910/d168744de x991.htm

To understand the challenge of being the CEO of a private company, I created the model below. Remember that, as George E.P. Box says, 'All models are wrong, but some are useful.' The model and explanations below will enable you to locate the stage of evolution your business has achieved.

At what stage is your business?

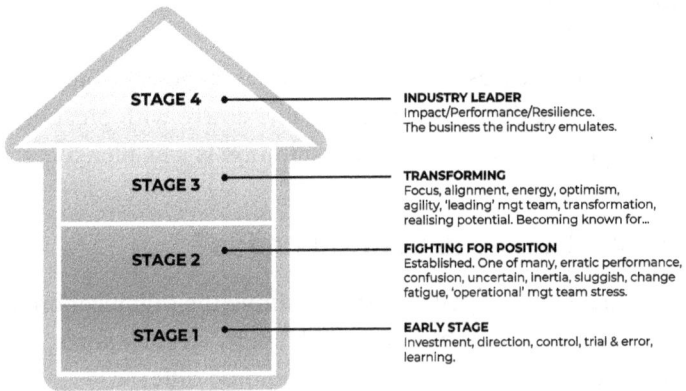

STAGE 4 — **INDUSTRY LEADER**
Impact/Performance/Resilience.
The business the industry emulates.

STAGE 3 — **TRANSFORMING**
Focus, alignment, energy, optimism, agility, 'leading' mgt team, transformation, realising potential. Becoming known for...

STAGE 2 — **FIGHTING FOR POSITION**
Established. One of many, erratic performance, confusion, uncertain, inertia, sluggish, change fatigue, 'operational' mgt team stress.

STAGE 1 — **EARLY STAGE**
Investment, direction, control, trial & error, learning.

FIGURE 1 At what stage is your business?

Stage 1. Early Stage

That exciting stage when you're starting out, building a team, building a brand—when every new customer is celebrated with a high five. An intense adrenaline rush characterises this stage. The CEO's role here is most likely to be directive, ensuring that the focus remains on what must be done among the myriad things that need to get done.

Stage 2. Fighting for Position

This is the most challenging position where organisations can be locked in a whirlpool. The business is well established, with loyal customers and an established brand, but it is not breaking through. Performance is erratic, and there is high stress in the organisation. The business model may be challenged. The bench strength of the management team is not quite there. Using a sporting analogy, for the CEO, this is like being the coach of the under-12s soccer team; you win some matches but lose many. Some star performers are on your team, but others secretly wish they were playing tennis! I would argue that many private companies stay locked in this stage and never break free. They bounce from opportunity to challenge to opportunity, but it is as if gravity is holding them back.

Stage 3. Transforming Organisation

This is an organisation that has broken out of Fighting for Position. They have the right team on the bus. They understand how they differentiate in the market; they have the right culture and are executing their strategic plan. Things are imperfect but responsive; they are learning from the market and their successes and failures. They have built the right team of external advisers. Continuing the sports coach analogy, for the CEO, this is like coaching the under-16s; everyone is there because they want to win, are talented and open to learning, and have the best coaching team!

Stage 4. Industry Leader

An organisation that has achieved transformation and knows how to reinvent. This organisation is resilient. It is the business the rest of the industry wants to be like. It does not mean they are the largest or necessarily the most profitable, but they are seen to be having the greatest impact. They can grow and continue to reinvent.

If you are reading this, I suspect you are currently somewhere in the Fighting for Position stage. You are seeking a way to break out and get to the next stage of evolution. You are in the right place.

So, as the business evolves at each level, the people, skills and resources required also differ. Some people will grow and evolve with the business and continue to lead; others will reach the summit of their capability or the limit of their passion to transform. They may find other roles in the organisation or move on to others.

When responding to the challenge of trying to break through the stages of growth, you know what you know, and you have a good sense of what you need to know to make better decisions, but then there is the issue of what you *don't know that you need to know.*

'The importance of being able to benefit from the wisdom of others and overcome those "blind spots" has a value that cannot be underestimated.'

CEO SURVEY RESPONDENT[3]

Your ambition has grown, and you're feeling held back. You want to break out to the next stage of growth. Still, the framework of support and advice you have now, be that a business coach, a consultant, your informal network of good friends with whom you confide periodically, or the peer-to-peer support group you are in, is not providing the thinking, commitment, or rigour you now need. Something needs to change.

---

3 In October 2020, I conducted a 'Lead Your Industry' survey of 33 private company CEOs and advisers. All CEO survey respondent quotes are from this survey.

It's likely that you already know you need to upscale the bandwidth of your leadership team. New skills and new thinking are needed. There are various incremental to radical options to restructure the team. Your team has been loyal and has contributed greatly to getting the business where it is now. You want to do the right thing for the business and the right thing for the team, and you are wrestling with finding the balance. You can envision an extended period of change but can't explore all restructuring options with your leadership team.

The same is true of your executive shareholders, as some of their roles may need to change. With whom can you have these conversations? Many people can have an opinion on these issues, but who has the relevant experience, expertise, objectivity and understanding of what is required to drive the strategic direction of the business? These are all signs that you're ready for change.

CASE STUDY
STREET FURNITURE AUSTRALIA

Street Furniture Australia (SFA) is an Australian manufacturing and innovation success story. They are recognised by their peers as industry leaders. The following is an extract from an article published in June 2018 in the Australian Institute of Company Directors (AICD) magazine, *Company Director*, that exemplifies what it is like to break out of Fighting for Position.

> Two years ago, SFA set up an external Advisory Board to allow the pair to maintain a focus on innovation and develop a broader business perspective.

Conybeare and Morrison (founders and directors) first engaged Anthony Moss GAICD to help the company develop a strategic plan so that it could become as forward-looking as possible.

'Through that process, the team became increasingly empowered; the management team became refined in terms of having the right people and the right fit,' says (MD) Morrison.

'The strategic planning process called for the directors to step back a little to give the senior management team a greater sense of authority and responsibility. The team had to step up and interact as a group of managers. In the process, it became obvious if there was a poor fit, and the team developed to become a refined and coordinated unit,' he says.

The (Advisory) board also includes accountant Peter Vickers, business consultant Blair Saddington, CM+ practice director Richard Dinham and landscape consultant Oi Choong.

Moss says an Advisory Board can provide support with governance, accountability, external expertise, and mentoring. 'One of the opportunities for an Advisory Board is to assist the directors in developing a broader perspective around the potential of their organisation to identify its blind spots. It also gives them confidence about where they want to put their focus and effort.'[4]

Since this article was published, Street Furniture Australia has launched multiple new product ranges that are dominating their market in Australia. They have built a robust

---

4   https://www.aicd.com.au/leadership/types/business-entrepreneurs/street-furniture.html

export business with a significant presence now in the USA and have recently achieved the status of being the first Australian street furniture manufacturer to achieve full 100% carbon neutral status certified by Climate Active™.

Street Furniture's Advisory Board has evolved since the article quoted a change in personnel and is now focused on the organisation's next step, which is a change in growth.

'Since establishing an Advisory Board under the chairmanship of Anthony Moss, our manufacturing business has benefited in many ways. We have been able to hold a mirror up to our whole operation, see our strong points and weaknesses, and make considerable judgements on how to improve.'

WILLIAM MORRISON
Managing Director, Street Furniture Australia

This case study highlights both the value and flexibility of an Advisory Board. The value of having the right advisers at the right time with the flexibility to transform as the business requirements evolve.

In summary, the success of any business depends on the capabilities of the CEO. How do you feel about your capabilities as CEO? Use the following questionnaire and exercise to determine where you might be experiencing opportunities for growth or change.

QUESTIONS FOR REFLECTION

	Rate your experience as CEO from one to ten in response to these questions, with ten being the highest and one being the lowest.	Rating* 1–10
1	Am I Commercially Lonely?	
2	Am I Constructively Discontent?	
3	Do I have the right skills to lead my organisation through the next growth stage?	
4	Does my leadership team have the necessary bench strength to implement a new strategy?	
5	How urgently does my business need to break out of this stage?	
6	How urgently do I need to change my support network that helps me think objectively about the business?	
7	How effective is my business at learning and upskilling?	

*10 = high

SCORESHEET

For Questions 1 and 2, any score of seven or above suggests an opportunity to change. For Questions 3 to 7, anything below seven suggests a need to change.

EXERCISE: IS THE TIME RIGHT NOW?

1   If you continue at the current rate of change, what will the business look like in three years? How will you feel at that point?

_____

e.g. is the current rate of change/growth exciting, challenging, adequate or inadequate?

_____

2   What's holding you back? If you could achieve just fifty per cent of the changes you seek to make, what would be the return for revenue, profit, cash and your time over the next three years? How would you feel at that point?

_____

e.g. is it cash, skills, people or resources?

_____

3   Other than appointing an Advisory Board vested in your and your business's success, what other catalyst might drive change? How likely is that to happen?

_____

e.g. hiring specific skills into the leadership team, hiring a business coach, or appointing a board of directors?

_____

2

Pathways
for Change

*The skills and mindset of the CEO
are Key Performance Indicators of an
organisation's capability to grow...*

With the desire to propel her company to greater heights,
Sarah made a momentous decision; she formed an Advisory Board comprising experts from diverse fields.

As the Advisory Board convened for their first meeting, Sarah felt a mix of excitement and anticipation. The members brought an array of perspectives, knowledge and networks to complement Sarah's strategic goals. The board consisted of a tech industry veteran and a celebrated sustainability advocate.

Each board member provided invaluable insights into cutting-edge technologies, emerging market trends, and potential disruptions that could shape the company's future. Their collective wisdom empowered Sarah to make well-informed decisions, mitigate risks and uncover new growth opportunities.

The Advisory Board acted as a formidable network for Sarah's company. Each member boasted extensive connections in their respective domains, opening doors to potential collaborations. Tom, the prominent tech industry expert on the board, was so impressed by the company's vision that he decided to invest, infusing Sarah's company with fresh capital.

Sarah also noticed that the mere presence of the board motivated her executive team to excel. The knowledge that the board would scrutinise their strategies and decisions spurred the team to be more accountable and proactive in their roles.

As Sarah ventured into new markets and faced challenges, the Advisory Board became her trusted confidant team. She sought their advice during crucial junctures, benefiting from their unbiased perspectives. Their guidance cultivated a continuous learning and innovation culture, enabling the company to adapt swiftly to changing market conditions.

As time passed, the Advisory Board became more than just a group of advisers; they became Sarah's allies and mentors. Their commitment to the company's success transcended board meetings, as they offered guidance and support whenever Sarah needed it.

Sarah's company soared to new heights under the Advisory Board's influence in a few short years. Revenue skyrocketed, reputation soared, and it became a beacon of innovation in the tech world. Sarah's decision to appoint the Advisory Board was a transformative moment in the company's journey.

Ultimately, the Advisory Board elevated Sarah's company and empowered her as a visionary leader. She embraced collaboration, sought counsel from experts, and instilled a culture of growth and adaptability within her company. The benefits Sarah derived from the Advisory Board extended far beyond the company's success—they transformed her into a more astute and confident CEO.

We've established that a key function of the CEO is to inspire the people in an organisation. You are the visionary, the leader, the driver, the final arbiter, and the ultimate decision-maker. In many ways, you are an organisation's greatest asset. As the leader of your company, you need the right support to always be able to play your best game.

You can accept incremental growth and incremental change, or you can choose to fast-track change. There are many options to fast-track change, including:

- investing time and money in training courses,

- investing significantly upfront by hiring new talent with the skills needed for the future,

- appointing a board of directors, or

- bringing in qualified consultants to address specific issues.

All these solutions are valid and will affect the rate of organisational change. Each option has implications regarding speed of impact, cost or control. Investing in training, for example, is likely to have a slower and perhaps less impactful effect than hiring in the required skills. Hiring to fill skill gaps (to build strategic financial capability into the business) is likely to be faster than training internal staff but is much more expensive. Appointing a board of directors with non-executives with the right skills comes at the expense of changing the dynamics of control of the business.

Your job is to choose the right pathway for your organisation based on your appetite for growth and risk.

What if there was a way to access the right mix of skills when needed? A team with deep capability in the areas that your organisation needs to develop who are vested in your success. A team that, because they are accessible on an as-needed basis, is far less costly than hiring the same resource full-time. And you get to choose whether to take and implement that advice.

This solution differs from all the other options in providing the right resources and flexibility; it is the CEO Game Changer—your Advisory Board.

The CEO's mindset is gold; it's one of the company's most significant intangible assets. What the CEO does and does not do permeates the organisation and will directly impact performance. When the CEO has more experience and greater capability, the potential for the company changes. It's like changing the lens on a camera from a standard lens to a zoom lens that can see further and wider. Suddenly, what did not seem possible is clearly within reach.

So, how do you fast-track the CEO's learning to fill that gap in experience or skills?

I contend that an Advisory Board with the right advisers and the right strategy can fast-track organisational change. When you assemble the right team of advisers, you create an A-team that has your back and appreciates the impact of you being the best you can be. Your A-team is vested in your success and understands your ambition for the business and the constraints and inertia you need to overcome. Your A-team will support and challenge you to rise further than you previously thought possible. They will provide frank and fearless advice, give tough love, and tell you what no one in your organisation can say. Your Advisory Board is focused on building you up for success that your business can follow.

> 'We have gained through improved strategy and more accountability and ensured the tough conversations are being held.'
>
> **CEO SURVEY RESPONDENT**

The model below highlights the transformational impact over time on the mindset of the CEO with the right Advisory Board.

On the left, we see the typical experience of the Commercially Lonely and discontented CEO described in the introduction. The CEO feels the weight of exertion as they have to push the business through the stages of growth. On the right, the CEO's focus transitions from exertion and control, driving the sense of pushing the business forward to being focused on and articulating the potential or pulling the business forward.

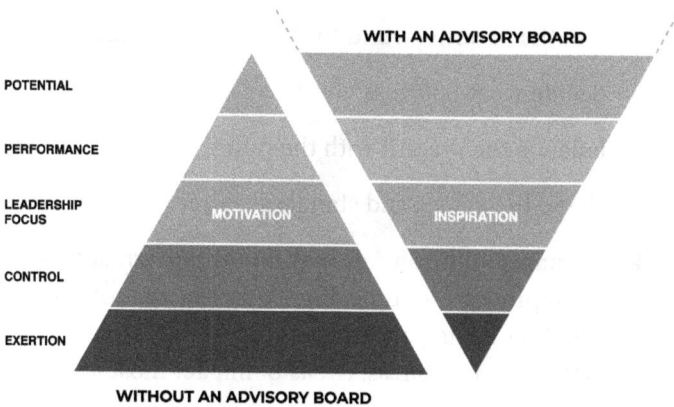

FIGURE 2 With and without an Advisory Board

Let's explore the model from left to right, starting at the base.

- **Exertion:** Without an Advisory Board, the exertion to push the business forward is high. With an Advisory Board, the sense of personal exertion required to drive change is reduced as the CEO knows they are not alone and has access to the right skills. This causes a multiplier effect on the CEO's efforts.

- **Control:** With an Advisory Board providing additional oversight, the CEO's need for control is reduced. When the control reflex is diminished, space is created to allow the leadership to develop organisational capability and resilience.

- **Leadership Focus:** With an Advisory Board, the CEO's leadership style can shift from being focused on motivation (driving action through external reward) to inspiration (stimulating change through intrinsic desire) to achieve shared goals. The CEO is released to focus on, as management guru Peter Drucker reportedly said, 'only what the CEO can do', and refined further by A.G. Lafley from the same source:

  - link the external world to the internal organisation

  - decide what business you are in

  - balance the present with the future

  - shape the values and standards of the organisation.

- **Performance:** With an Advisory Board, performance inevitably improves over time. Eighty-six per cent of leaders believe that having an Advisory Board has significantly impacted their business. Areas of impact most cited are company vision, innovation, risk management and profitability. The speed of change the board can help drive is limited only by the organisation's hunger for change, the priorities set, and the resources the CEO applies.

* **Potential**: With an Advisory Board, the CEO sees greater potential for the business; what was once a possibility becomes a probability. As probability changes, the appetite for the magnitude and/or speed of success can also change along with the strategic priorities.

With an Advisory Board acting as a coach, mentor and expert advisory team, the CEO has a support structure that empowers them with the right mindset and skill set to be the best they can be. This translates to better decisions and leadership that ultimately leads to better performance and is the key to transcending your business's Fighting for Position stage.

Potential restrained

The previous model highlighted the impact of an Advisory Board on the mindset and focus of the CEO. The model below (Figure 3) looks at your business and how restraints withholding growth need to be overcome. You have your team of people, your resources (financial, systems, operations) and leadership team. You have an ambition for the business, a picture of success, and a clear strategic direction. However, your business cannot outperform the capability of your leadership. The hard edges of the boundaries in the triangle structure below restrain your perspective on the business's potential.

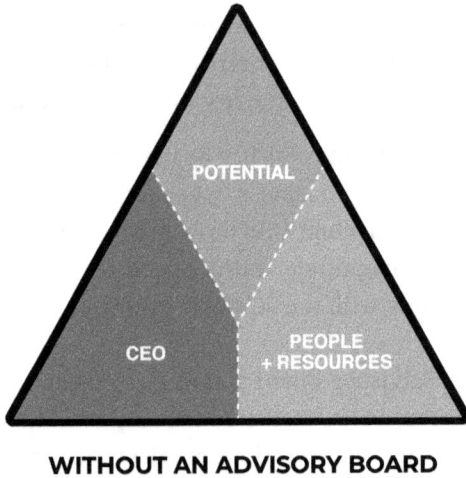

WITHOUT AN ADVISORY BOARD

FIGURE 3 Potential restrained

You can intuitively see the opportunity for the business and the impediments holding you back from achieving your vision. While you may have good people around you, you have various capabilities. Some have helped you grow to this point but probably don't have the skills for where you want to take the business, and perhaps newer team members have tremendous potential but are unproven. You may have funding constraints; growing a business requires more working capital. You have resource challenges like manufacturing capacity, supply chain issues, or office space. You address all these factors as your capability allows, but the business is restrained. You are aware that if you could fast-track solutions to these issues, you could achieve the business's potential much more swiftly.

Potential unleashed

Imagine if the boundaries holding your business back, keeping it in Fighting for Position, could shift from being hard edges to being more permeable or even removed entirely. Appointing an Advisory Board with members with the right skills removes the limitations that restrain your business.

With the restraints dissipated, the CEO can see the potential for the business at an entirely new level. The model below (Figure 4) illustrates the impact of potential unleashed.

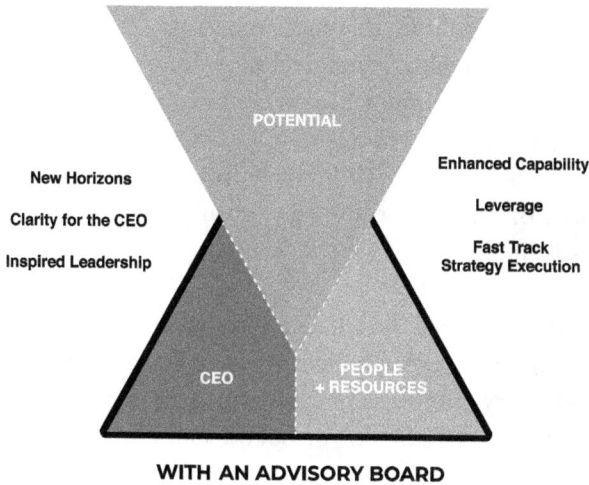

New Horizons

Clarity for the CEO

Inspired Leadership

POTENTIAL

Enhanced Capability

Leverage

Fast Track
Strategy Execution

CEO

PEOPLE
+ RESOURCES

WITH AN ADVISORY BOARD

FIGURE 4 Potential Unleashed

The left-hand side of the model highlights the benefits for the CEO, and on the right-hand side, the long-term benefits of an Advisory Board that accrue for the organisation.

Benefits for the CEO

With unrestricted potential, the CEO can envision new, expanded horizons and previously unseen or deemed unattainable opportunities.

There is never enough time in the day for the CEO. That, of course, is a mindset issue, but the pressure is real. Dwight D. Eisenhower once said, 'I have two kinds of problems: the urgent and the important. The urgent are not important, and the important are never urgent.'

In response to this challenge, he created what is now known as the Eisenhower Matrix—a mapping tool to identify if a decision is urgent and important.

A CEO must make myriad decisions, and the pressure will always be on the urgent. This is because urgent, less important decisions are often easier to make. Having an Advisory Board puts a framework in place to ensure every meeting focuses on the important but non-urgent. This clarity of focus is liberating for a CEO, who can be dragged into the business's minutiae.

With a laser focus on what's important, the CEO becomes a better, inspiring leader, building their team and releasing that discretionary effort that powers extraordinary achievement.

As the CEO, where do you spend your time?

The 'do decide' delegate model

	Urgent	NOT Urgent
Important	Do	Decide
NOT Important	Delegate	Delete

FIGURE 5 Eisenhower Matrix

Benefits for the business

A fundamental role of an Advisory Board is to build the organisation's capability. This can be achieved directly by appointing Advisory Board members with the specific skills needed that the organisation cannot yet hire in, assisting the CEO to bring in the right consultants at the right time, directly mentoring the CEO and leadership team, and potentially improving access to capital.

Fast-track strategy execution

Enhanced capability inevitably leads to the ability to fast-track the execution of your strategy, whether through better skills, a sharper focus on the key strategic initiatives, or just figuring out a better, faster, less resource-intensive way of operating.

Leverage

Enhanced capability, leading to fast-tracked strategy execution, enables an organisation to leap forward, skipping real or perceived hurdles. That leverage can manifest in many ways, including increased market penetration, brand equity, improved profitability, faster new product development, enhanced innovation, and more.

Sounds pretty good, right?

REFLECTION

Building Leadership Capability or Bench Strength that leads to better performance is the key to transcending your business's Fighting for Position stage:

How strongly and how urgently do you want to break out of your business's Fighting for Position stage?

When is the right time to change?

I have been a member of a community called Thought Leaders.[5] It's a community of professionals who run a practice sharing their expertise. This community has been an invaluable source of inspiration and a great support network for me for several years. The irony is that some five years before I joined Thought Leaders, a mentor of mine recommended I join this group. It took me five years to make that decision. My practice, Lead Your Industry Pty Ltd, would have positively impacted so many more businesses if I had heeded that sage advice five years earlier.

How many times in the life of your business have you considered taking a certain action only to delay that decision, perhaps because the gain was not clear, or the pain of avoidance was not great enough? Then, at some point in the future, you did make that decision, you took that action, and almost immediately afterwards, you kicked yourself, saying, 'Why, oh why, didn't I make that decision sooner?'

So, how do you know when it is the right time to appoint an Advisory Board?

For an Advisory Board structure to be relevant and impactful, your business needs to be of sufficient scale or complexity and have sufficient management bandwidth. The Advisory Board can only advise. It does not execute. So, sufficient internal capability and resources are needed to execute the plan effectively. For smaller businesses (a start-up, for example), the CEO or directors must have an appetite to drive growth fast and be willing to apply resources accordingly.

---

5   https://www.thoughtleaders.com.au

Remember, an Advisory Board is a potential game changer for the CEO, so the primary determinant is the appetite and urgency with which the CEO wants to change the business's current trajectory. Clear signposts indicate that it may be the right time to appoint your Advisory Board.

For example, imagine a CEO running a business for over five years. There has been growth, and the business is profitable, but it is definitely stuck in the Fighting for Position mode. The CEO has several ideas on breaking out but believes that the leadership team, which is full of good people who are best described as operational leaders, does not have the skills or experience to drive the new initiatives effectively. This is creating inertia. In this instance, an Advisory Board can assist the CEO in testing the new initiatives, evaluate the leadership team's capability (including the CEO), and support the CEO's confidence in taking the most appropriate next steps.

'I needed to find a way to educate my executive peers, include them in decision-making, reduce the resistance to change, and have a forum for listening to them better. They (the Advisory Board) became allies and helped me with the transformation.'

CEO SURVEY RESPONDENT

Common signposts that highlight the circumstances could warrant an Advisory Board include:

1   Externally driven need for change

A company facing volatile change, where either a multitude of opportunities and strategic choices need to be made, or several new threats need to be mitigated.

For example, in early 2020, when COVID-19 spread across the globe and lockdowns ensued, many businesses were either forced to close or mothball. Even if they were not forced to close, the channel to their end-user was closed. How does a CEO respond to such a situation? Faced with such existential threats, an Advisory Board can provide the skills, objective perspective, and appropriate decision-making framework to enable the CEO to again make confident decisions, both tactically and strategically.

2   Leading up to, or shortly after, a change in equity

For example, during a longer-term exit strategy, there is typically a need to build organisational maturity and rigour into the business, particularly where a founder seeks to exit. Often, there needs to be an investment in people, brand, intellectual property protection, and systems to maximise the value of a potential purchase. An Advisory Board can provide guidance through this process. Often, after a significant change in equity, there may be a change in CEO, the strategy, or other key leaders in the organisation. The new shareholders/directors can have a different appetite for growth; they may wish to move faster or slower, more aggressively or more conservatively. An Advisory Board can fill the skills gap identified via the strategic planning process.

3 There is a need to manage difficult conversations at the highest level

Difficult conversations within a leadership team or between directors or shareholders can be a huge source of inertia. Consider the scenario where two shareholding directors, each owning fifty per cent, have a common vision but a different perspective on strategy or execution. The business can be hamstrung on issues where an agreement cannot be reached. The result can be, at best, inertia that holds the business back. At worst, if positions are intractable, the business may be wound up. An Advisory Board can objectively navigate difficult conversations and enable decisions, freeing the business to move forward.

4 There is a desire or need to improve governance but not an appetite to appoint independent non-executive directors

There may be an appetite to establish a more rigorous governance framework to improve decision-making, address multiple stakeholder interests, build organisational maturity, ensure regulatory requirements are met, or meet investor requirements. However, at the same time, there may not be an interest in appointing non-executive directors to ensure no dilution of control. The Advisory Board, while not a governance structure, can give the CEO perspective and a framework of appropriate steps to take and their relative impact.

5 It is a family businesses

Family businesses can be complex. There is often tension between the leader's role as executive and their role as a family member. That tension can be amplified if there is a mix of family and non-family members at the executive level.

Family businesses can benefit from an Advisory Board's objectivity in working through these tensions.

Occasionally, the CEO can start to doubt their capability. They have been successful but now recognise that new skills are needed. Are they the right person to take the business to the next level? An Advisory Board can help the CEO work through this dilemma by providing mentoring or working through alternative solutions.

The CEO who appoints an Advisory Board should relish the opportunity it provides and the accountability it requires. If that sounds like you, then you probably have a thirst to succeed, matched with a thirst to learn from those with the skills and experience you don't have. This is just the right mindset you need to embark on your Advisory Board journey.

QUESTIONS FOR REFLECTION

1   How is your business restrained from realising its full potential?

2   What does success look like for you?

3   How do you, the CEO, add the greatest value to the business, and how much time do you spend on those value-adding activities daily and weekly?

4   With whom do you discuss those issues that are undiscussable with your people and leaders? If you could afford to add a specific capability that would significantly enhance your ability to execute your strategy, what would it be?

5   If you had the right Advisory Board already in place, in board meetings, what aspects of the business would you spend most of your time talking about?

PART TWO

THE GAME CHANGER

3

How Does an Advisory Board Work?

*So, what is an Advisory Board, and how
does it differ from other advisory structures?*

BEFORE I DESCRIBE in more detail what an Advisory Board is, let's clarify what an Advisory Board is *not*. An Advisory Board is not the board of directors of your company. An Advisory Board is not a legally defined entity with any control or veto power over the decision-making authority of the CEO or directors. Members of an Advisory Board are not shadow directors as defined by the Corporations Act (Australia). An Advisory Board is not the sole source of advice available to CEOs.

Now that we're clear on what it is not, let's look at what it is. My definition of an Advisory Board is as follows:

An Advisory Board is a small group of professionals, each with a specific skill set and relevant commercial experience. The board has a commercial focus and empowers the

CEO to achieve the goals that he/she sets for the business by making better, more informed decisions.

The Advisory Board achieves this by providing independent, objective advice and support but also challenges the CEO's thinking. An Advisory Board tests the organisation's ambition by exploring alternatives that may yield greater, faster growth and/or profitability while being mindful of the organisation's resources and risk appetite.

Typically, the Advisory Board's areas of focus include, but are not limited to:

- the potential for the organisation and the vision that has been set
- the validity of the strategy and business model to achieve the vision
- the skills and capability of the CEO and leaders to achieve the goals
- the resources required, including financial, people and technical, and how to access those resources efficiently
- the execution of the strategic plan
- accountability for the CEO
- evaluation of the performance of the business versus its potential

Let's get granular about the benefits of an Advisory Board with the right advisers who have the right skills.

A safe and confidential sounding board for the CEO

'The Advisory Board also helps avoid CEO isolation. You can pick up the phone to chew over an idea or a problem with that wise external party who has a strong vested interest.'

CEO SURVEY RESPONDENT

Earlier, I described CEOs who are Commercially Lonely. When independent advisers are appointed to the Advisory Board, it becomes a forum where the CEO can discuss any issue of concern—particularly those that cannot be discussed with other staff members. These conversations might relate to strategies that will impact business performance, employment, leadership team capability, and even the navigation of difficult conversations with fellow shareholders/directors.

The CEO can explore and discuss potential initiatives without judgement. The Advisory Board can challenge, support, and offer alternative ideas that the CEO can consider. This is about ensuring that the CEO is focused on the important and not the urgent-unimportant. That said, the CEO retains control. Seeking the counsel of the Advisory Board does not mean that advice binds the CEO. The CEO is free to decide the course of action.

Objectivity

A CEO can't be objective about the business, strategy, potential and capability. Think about asking the Prime Minister to rate their performance—they can't do it objectively. The CEO is inevitably biased, not least because they are emotionally and financially entangled with the business: the business is the creation of the CEO, and they see its success or failure as fundamental to who they are as a person. Plus, when they are also a shareholder, their family's wealth depends upon the business's success.

CEOs are human and have cognitive biases, whether it's a bias for action, confirmation bias (only looking for evidence that confirms their perspective) or loss aversion. CEOs see problems and opportunities and how to respond to them through the lens of their particular biases.

Contrast this with the fact that an Advisory Board is by default objective. It is emotionally detached from the organisation but holds the success of the CEO and the business as its core reason for being. The Advisory Board can, therefore, provide objective counsel and alternative perspectives. It enables the CEO to see how their natural bias impacts their decision-making: for example, hiring executives like themselves or not validating gut decisions to the detriment of themselves and the business. The Advisory Board is that 'sense-check' for CEO decision-making that a leadership team typically cannot provide.

Accountability

Who is the CEO accountable to? If you are running your own business, it's easy to change your direction or do something more slowly or quickly than perhaps originally planned. That's okay, except when you change your commitments for the wrong reasons or when a change of mind negatively impacts your leadership team and other employees.

How can your leadership team be accountable if you are not accountable for your commitments? Being accountable isn't just about the 'stick'. It's about validating and sharing commitments before they're made, which tells your team what is important and brings them on the journey.

The Advisory Board must be in lockstep with the CEO over the strategic direction. Once confirmed, the Advisory Board 'owns' the strategy and is there to assist the CEO with the fast-track execution of the business strategy. The Advisory Board also ensures that the CEO evaluates new opportunities and challenges through the lens of the potential impact on the strategy.

'The monthly rhythm to prepare a board pack and review performance is something that wouldn't happen with such consistency without (the Advisory Board meetings).'

CEO SURVEY RESPONDENT

An Advisory Board ensures the CEO maintains perspective, stays focused and is less distracted than they might otherwise be.

New thinking

Your advisers need to think differently from you. Your perspective is based on your life experience and your expertise. There's a good chance that some, if not all, of your leadership team members think like you do. Your Advisory Board can be the source of different thinking, pushing the boundaries of your collective field of vision. The Advisory Board's diversity of thought enables the CEO's thinking to break free from the shackles of a limited perspective and explore possibilities of greater ambition for the business.

Enhanced capability

The strategic planning process may have identified a critical skill gap. Adding an Advisory Board member with deep expertise in that area (e.g., digital marketing, strategic finance, global supply chain management, etc.) can provide access to the necessary new skills. This provides access to a level of capability beyond what the organisation would consider normal for its level of maturity. For example, an organisation may see the need for a CFO with global strategic financial skills but cannot provide sufficient stimulation for a full-time person. Appointing such a person to the Advisory Board provides 'access' to those skills as needed.

Access to networks (the little black book)

Your Advisory Board members will all bring their 'little black book' of business contacts. These contacts can provide access to target market segments or international markets. They can also provide access to a supplier network of tried and tested goods or services that are fit for purpose. Your Advisory Board's collective black book dramatically speeds up your access to the right networks.

Governance

By its nature, an Advisory Board establishes a level of governance, notwithstanding the fact the Advisory Board exists at the pleasure of the CEO. Having structured meetings with an agenda and note-taking, where stakeholders' interests, strategic direction, performance and people management are all explored, is a form of governance. This is not to the level that the directors of the organisation are held to in accordance with Corporations Law. Advisory Boards are not required to establish a governance framework, but the issues they explore inevitably impact the CEO and their thinking about the governance structure within the organisation that can highlight any blind spots.

Clarity for the CEO

'The benefits are enormous; you really get to work on your business rather than in your business for that day.'

CEO SURVEY RESPONDENT

When surrounded by their A-team, the CEO can clearly see the organisation's enhanced capability and potential. Among the myriad things the CEO has to address, their focus becomes sharper on the key strategic issues, and their leadership style shifts from motivation (driving performance through external reward) to inspiration (eliciting drive from within).

Improved performance

Of course, performance improvements will vary from business to business. Still, a 2014 study by the Business Development Bank of Canada compared the financial performance of a group of companies that engaged an Advisory Board with a pool of businesses that didn't engage an Advisory Board. The study showed improved performance between those with and those without an Advisory Board, as well as improved performance pre- and post-appointment of an Advisory Board.

The quote below highlights just some of the results.[6]

In fact, 86% of leaders believe that having an Advisory Board has had a significant impact on the success of their business. Areas of impact most often cited are company vision, innovation, risk management and profitability... From 2001 to 2011, the average annual sales of businesses with Advisory Boards were 24% higher than those of comparable companies. Moreover, productivity was 18% higher on average over the same period. (BDC, 2014 p. 1)

The survey also captured the main obstacle to establishing an Advisory Board. 'The main reason they have not done so (set up an Advisory Board) is the belief that it involves too much work, time and effort.'

In September 2020, I decided to conduct my own study about Advisory Boards by reaching out to clients and colleagues for their perspectives to identify the benefits and challenges.

Of thirty-two respondents, eighty-seven per cent of survey participants recommended establishing an Advisory Board. Many respondents described the experience of engaging an Advisory Board as highly valuable.[7]

---

6   https://www.bdc.ca/en/Documents/analysis_research/bdc_study_advisory_boards.pdf

7   The survey questions are in Appendix 1 at the end of this book.

CASE STUDY
TIGER TRIBE

Naomi and Anthony Green founded their business Tiger Tribe in 2007 to design gifts and toys that tap into a child's imagination and sense of fun. Whether developing a new skill, mastering a technique, increasing independence, or making fun family memories, Tiger Tribe products nurture confidence and creativity in kids.

The business has grown significantly, supplying gift and specialty toy stores across Australia and through distributors across the globe. Their most recent success has been establishing a subsidiary in the US to closely manage their market penetration.

The following is an extract from an article in the AICD magazine, *Company Director*, in April 2021.[8]

Creating an Advisory Board helped Tiger Tribe's founders tackle strategic challenges and stimulate growth. An informal Advisory Board began meeting sporadically in 2011. It included Anthony and Naomi, plus Ted Russell, a retired former mining company CFO who was also a mentor to Naomi in financial management, along with Naomi's father Colin Wise, the former general counsel of a mining company.

The Advisory Board meetings became a regular occurrence when Tiger Tribe received a federal government grant in 2014 to subsidise strategic business adviser Anthony Moss. 'As we grew, we needed help with facing the next set of challenges—ones that were beyond our current knowledge base,' explains Naomi. 'We see the Advisory Board as helping us with the things we don't know yet.'

---

8   https://www.aicd.com.au/news-media/company-director-magazine/all-editions/april-2021-edition.html

The Advisory Board began as a way of measuring whether the company was achieving its strategic objectives—one of which was to export its products. A roadmap was created and someone with expertise in exports was recruited.

Having an Advisory Board was crucial in a time of heightened anxiety when COVID-19 broke out in Australia in March 2020, the Greens say.

'A year ago, when none of us had any idea whether COVID-19 would decimate us, we called an emergency Advisory Board meeting. It was a great help for calming our nerves and focusing on short-term plans that helped us stay on track,' says Naomi.

Since this article was published, Tiger Tribe's leadership team and their Advisory Board have evolved to include two additional members with finance and global distribution experience.

What are alternative options for support?

If you have read this far, I suspect you recognise that having a support network to help you become a better CEO is essential. Of course, an Advisory Board is not the only option available to support CEOs in their roles, but it does provide unique benefits that alternative solutions may not. Here are some other options available for CEOs feeling Commercially Lonely and Constructively Discontent:

Executive coach

If you've never had one, start here. Every successful athlete has a coach, and so should you. An experienced coach will uncover your blind spots and help you discover your strengths and weaknesses, how you can develop, and what impact that will have. The Executive Coach's focus is on helping the CEO be more effective.

Consultant/business coach

Business Coaches or consultants are typically brought into an organisation to address specific issues, such as strategy, systems, people development, and so forth. Normally, these relationships are transactional and end when the specific project is complete.

Business mentor

Mentors are successful business professionals. Their role is to share their experience of successes and failures. Mentors can be a great source of advice in the early stages of a business.

Peer-to-peer CEO groups

Peer-to-peer CEO groups are typically small groups of CEOs who come together periodically to learn from and share with each other. Each CEO, along with the Chair, contributes to the group's learning. This is an ideal glimpse of an Advisory Board experience. The key differences are that there is inevitably limited time to spend on your business issues, you did not choose your fellow members, and they may not have domain-relevant experience. See details of my CEO Advisory Board at the end of the book.

Appointing your own Advisory Board, by its nature, means you hand-pick your advisers, ensuring the relevance of your experience and spending 100% of your meeting time on your organisation's issues.

Governance Board

In Australia, private companies must have at least one director who fulfils the governance function to ensure the company operates within the law and meets all compliance requirements. For this illustration, I have assumed appointing a Governance Board means appointing non-executive directors.

A Governance Board can have all the attributes of an Advisory Board, and it is the right step when an organisation's shareholders want greater rigour in overseeing the executive function and key stakeholder management. It is absolutely the right step as your business grows in size and complexity.

The key difference between a Governance Board and an Advisory Board is control. A Governance Board, while not running the company, exercises control over the CEO and the strategy. An Advisory Board exercises no control and is advisory only. Final decisions, including ignoring the Advisory Board, rest with the CEO.

The following table outlines the differences more explicitly.

Advisory Board	Governance Board
A group of advisers appointed at the pleasure of the CEO.	This includes non-executive directors who exercise control jointly with other directors.
Commercially focused. They empower the CEO to achieve their goals for the business.	Legal obligation to operate in the interests of the corporate entity itself.
The objective is to understand the strengths and weaknesses of the CEO and the organisation and provide a pathway to improve both.	Selects and evaluates the CEO, who can be replaced.
Makes the CEO aware of risks that they may not have considered. Risk appetite and tolerance are solely the responsibility of the CEO/directors.	Is directly liable for certain financial risks and criminal prosecution. It can drive a risk-averse orientation to decision-making.
*No legal liability is attached to an Advisory Board, provided it does not act as a shadow director. See below.	

Advisory Board	Governance Board
Enables private companies to have access to a wider talent pool, including those who would not be comfortable assuming the liabilities that flow from being a director.	Directors are typically executive shareholders or non-executive shareholders in private companies. It can be difficult to secure independent directors in these companies where control is concentrated and closely held.
For private companies, the Advisory Board can highlight an appropriate governance structure and the benefits directly beneficial to the CEO and the business.	A Governance Board is exactly that: it ensures an appropriate governance structure and accountabilities.
Advisory Board members are there exclusively for the CEO's pleasure and can be changed.	Directors are normally appointed for a specific term.
An Advisory Board is NOT a decision-making body. It has no control over the CEO/directors; it can only advise. The CEO and directors make all decisions, as they are all responsible for the implications of those decisions.	A Governance Board is a decision-making body. Depending on the structure of the board, it can compel the CEO to take certain actions.
Advisory Board members are appointed at the discretion of the CEO/directors and may serve short or long terms.	The shareholders appoint directors.

Summary	
It's ideal when the CEO wants to engage with committed experts, who can help develop the CEO and the business, but ultimately wants to retain control.	This is ideal as the business expands and greater rigour is required to hold the executive function accountable and manage key stakeholders.

*A shadow director is essentially someone who has influence on the board and decision-making but who is not officially appointed a director. For more information, see https://www.aicd.com.au/board-of-directors/roles/alternate/what-type-of-director-are-you.html

The right support framework depends on your unique CEO journey and appetite. This book is about the value an Advisory Board structure can deliver. Shift to an Advisory

Board when you have high ambition, are committed to driving growth, are open to learning from others, and are comfortable having your ideas challenged but do not have the appetite to relinquish complete control.

4

Building Your
Advisory Board

*Making it work, the right
people, the right process.*

LET'S IMAGINE the scenario of a manufacturing business
turning over some $24 million annually. The shareholders
are the three founders of the business; the current CEO
holds fifty per cent of the shares, and the others own twenty-
five per cent each. All three are directors listed on the ASIC
register.[9] In operation for more than ten years, the business
has identified opportunities in a complementary market
that could offer significant potential locally and the opportunity to expand internationally. Reaching the new market
will require additional machinery and technical capability investment. At the same time, the majority shareholder
has decided he wishes to exit the business in the next
twelve months.

---

9   https://asic.gov.au/ The Australian Securities and Investments Commission

The leadership team comprises three directors and three other managers who would best be described as operational. The organisation has a positive, supportive culture, but the CEO's skills and performance have led to a default mode of agreement with all the CEO's ideas and initiatives.

The shareholder directors meet quarterly, but these meetings tend to be short and focused on financial performance and dividend distribution.

An Advisory Board would be helpful in this scenario to:

- enable the CEO to become conscious of his/her biases and blind spots

- give the directors the space to be able to contribute ideas

- add the technical capability needed for the new growth strategy

- enable the CEO and directors to craft the right exit strategy

- assist the directors to fast-track strategy execution

- provide a safe environment to hold difficult conversations

- mentor the directors and management team members

The long-term impact of having an Advisory Board structure in this scenario is likely to:

- create new strategic opportunities

- eliminate the inertia of the leadership team

- improve performance

- foster better decisions

- inspire a succession plan

In short, the result will be a cohesive, high-performing team with a clear strategy that understands their capabilities, weaknesses and priorities. Of course, this does not mean it will be a perfect business with perfect results. It does not mean they may not receive significant shocks to their business, but it does mean that they will have been far more resilient in response to those shocks than if they had not had an Advisory Board.

CASE STUDY
CHARLIE'S FINE FOOD CO.

A case in point. During the initial stages of the COVID-19 pandemic in Australia, I chaired the Advisory Board of Charlie's Fine Food Co., which had been meeting quarterly. The lockdowns severely impacted the company's customers, and they had to make some very significant existential decisions in a short space of time. From March to May of that year, the Advisory Board met every two weeks. The organisation survived the shocks, re-focused and rebuilt the business.

Starting in April, fortnightly meetings were held remotely with the Advisory Board, which helped Magid and Mahlab, executive directors, steer their way through a complete strategy rethink. They had become all things to all customers, perhaps without a clear definition. The Advisory Board forced the directors to rethink why they were in business, what difference they wanted to make, who they wanted to serve, and what products they wanted. The result was a much narrower customer and product profile focusing on where they could add real value and distinguish themselves from competitors.[10]

---

10 For more details on this story, see AICD *Company Director* magazine, August 2020, or visit https://www.aicd.com.au/corporate-governance-sectors/small-business/growth/strategy-tips-for-business-owners-during-crisis.html

'We drafted a plan, and the Advisory Board repeatedly sent it back to us, saying, "Simple means five products, not fifty." It was really valuable to have that expertise and independent input.'

MAGID
Director, Charlie's Fine Food Co.

Typical structure of an Advisory Board

The typical Advisory Board consists of three professionals, one of whom is the Chair. To be clear, the Chair is *not* the CEO. Once the ground rules are set, the Advisory Board supports the CEO and does not need to be managed by the CEO. It is the Chair's role to manage each meeting to ensure it is meaningful, effective, and relevant for the CEO. This enables the CEO to participate fully in the substance of the meeting.

In the Advisory Board meetings, there is no-holds-barred discussion in the sense that all subjects are relevant and can be discussed within the context of an effective meeting.

Terms of Reference or Charter

It is important to clarify the terms of reference of the Advisory Board, which is typically called a Charter. The Charter sets out the reason for being on the Advisory Board, the expectations the organisation has of its adviser members, what success looks like, how appointments will be made, tenure and how members will be removed, the frequency of meetings, and how remuneration will be managed. Essentially, it's the framework of how the organisation will manage the Advisory Board.

Specific charters are unique to each organisation, but the table that follows shows the typical headings included.

Typical Advisory Board Charter headings

Heading	Meaning
Purpose (or role) of the Advisory Board	This section explains why the Advisory Board exists, who it's for and what success looks like.
Composition	Describes how members of the Advisory Board are chosen. The typical term of appointment, as well as confirmation appointments, is at will and can be terminated by the CEO at any time.
Meeting Format	The nature and frequency of meetings and the agenda format.
Compensation	Outlines the organisation's approach to compensation and expense management.
Confidentiality/ Conflict of Interest	Outlines the confidentiality agreement of the board.
Advisory Only	Clarifies the fact that the Advisory Board is an advisory body. Only the CEO/directors have sole responsibility for decision-making and implementation.
Evaluation	Describes how the effectiveness of the Advisory Board and its members will be evaluated. Typically, annually.

Frequency of meetings

Meetings can be held monthly, bi-monthly or quarterly. The meeting frequency is determined by:

1   The capability of the CEO and organisation to digest the ideas that emanate from each meeting.

2   The appetite of the CEO to drive change.

Monthly meetings can be appropriate in a larger organisation with a strong leadership team, ample resources readily available, and a high appetite to drive change.

Conversely, in a smaller or younger organisation with a more operational leadership team, it would be more relevant for the CEO to hold bi-monthly or quarterly meetings. This gives the CEO and the leadership team time to digest ideas and consider alternate sources of advice.

The speed at which the CEO seeks to drive growth or change will also influence the appropriate cadence of Advisory Board meetings. The Advisory Board may challenge the CEO's decision regarding speed, whether too fast or too slow.

Catalyst to change the meeting frequency

The meeting schedule needs to be flexible to respond to the business's commercial pressures, which can be external or internal.

Charlie's Fine Food Co. highlights how an external impact can dramatically influence the frequency of meetings. Other external factors may include a new regulatory environment or competitive threat. Internal shocks—for example, the resignation of a key person or funding challenges—can also result in the need for more frequent meetings as the CEO considers how best to respond.

Effective meetings

Based on my experience chairing many Advisory Board meetings, the most important framework is to determine intent. There must be a key point of discussion for the meeting.

The success of any meeting, of course, depends on preparation. The preparation for an Advisory Board meeting is driven by the Chair interacting with the CEO to determine the burning issues. The Chair's responsibility is to then manage the meeting to ensure sufficient time is allocated to the key issues. All meetings should have a period of reflection, assessing what's happened since the last meeting and the implications. There will be ongoing discussion points, like how the execution of the strategic plan rolled out. Then, there are longer-horizon issues, such as people development, succession, and significant market changes.

One of the key advantages of an Advisory Board is the in-built flexibility and the singular commercial focus of the board, namely, to enable the CEO and the business to be the best they can be. That translates in meetings to having the agility to adjust the agenda to the prevailing needs of the CEO and the business.

Meeting framework

Here is my recommended meeting framework:

- **Seven days before the meeting**: The Chair identifies up to three key issues for discussion with the CEO. The Chair then circulates the agenda along with the minutes of the last meeting as a reminder.

- **Five days before the meeting**: The CEO issues the management report, providing an overview of performance, decisions made and actions taken since the last meeting. It also includes any relevant commercial information about the business internally or external market conditions. The CEO (or CFO) also shares the up-to-date financial reports.

- **Meeting day**: Meeting dates will already have been blocked out for the year to ensure maximum attendance. Meetings will generally last between two and four hours, depending on the range of issues for discussion. They are ideally held away from the CEO's office to eliminate the distraction of normal commercial activities. The typical agenda for the day looks like this:

  - Updates since the last meeting
  - Review of year-to-date financial reports
  - Review CEO report
  - Discuss key issues: This is the crux of the meeting, and the most time should be allocated for this section

    - Issue 1
    - Issue 2
    - Issue 3

  - Any other business
  - Meeting summation and close

- **Actions/Minutes**: These should be brief, capturing the key points and the actions that the CEO has decided to take.

CEO retains control

A fundamental tenet of an Advisory Board is that the CEO retains control. The CEO controls who is on the board, how long they stay on the board, and how frequently the board meets. There is no voting process. The CEO makes all the decisions and determines the timing and allocation of resources. The Advisory Board is one source of advice, and there may well be occasions when the CEO obtains alternative advice contrary to what is received from the Advisory Board; the CEO alone makes the call.

Who should be on your Advisory Board

Consider this scenario. Katrina is the founder and CEO of a food industry business.

Her strategy is clear. Over the last eight years, she has built a business of substance, with a recognised brand and a key point of market differentiation. There are significant growth opportunities, and Katrina has a burning ambition for the business. Her strategy is set to grow through expansion into international markets, with an exit strategy via a trade sale in five years or so.

Katrina has decided to establish an Advisory Board; she knows there is much for her and her team to learn if she is to achieve her ambition. She has secured a Chair for the Advisory Board; Jim is a recently retired icon of the industry who built an international business before selling it to the market leader. He has a reputation for making the right moves.

Katrina knows she needs to improve internal systems and supply chain management, particularly as they expand internationally. She also knows that to make the business more attractive to a future buyer, she needs to extricate herself from being seen to be both the face and driving force of the business. She needs to build capability in her leadership team.

In discussion with the newly appointed Chair, they jointly decided an ideal appointment would be a senior partner in a major accounting firm that also provides outsourced CFO services. That person can provide the oversight of how the internal structure needs to develop over time to be fit for purpose and ensure the systems and financial management rigour are right at the point when Katrina wishes to exit. It just so happens Jim has worked with someone who fits that bill exactly. Katrina and Jim agree that having two external members on the Advisory Board is sufficient for the foreseeable future.

While this is a fictitious story it represents closely how the decision to appoint emerges and how the selection and appointment of Advisory Board members can occur.

Choose the Chair first

The Chair's role is to ensure the Advisory Board meets the desired outcomes for which it was created; hence, this role needs to be appointed first. The Chair then assists the CEO to secure additional members as needed.

You might seek a Chair that has deep market knowledge, experience in scaling businesses or specific technical expertise (e.g. finance, marketing, technology, etc.). However, the most important expertise they need is to be an effective Chair of the Advisory Board. That means they need to have experience on an Advisory Board or Governance Board, ideally as Chair. They need broad commercial experience and the maturity to understand that their job is to advise, not direct. They need the emotional intelligence to be able to work with the CEO and to understand the dynamics of what the CEO wants the Advisory Board to achieve. At the same time, they need to be able to offer frank and fearless advice, including (when necessary) pointing out to the CEO how their decision-making may be flawed, biased, or just not in their own interests.

So specifically, what does the Chair do?

- Ensures the CEO has clarified their ambition for the business and documented it in a strategic plan. If it hasn't been done, that's Step 1.

- Clarifies the purpose of the Advisory Board, its terms of reference and what is expected of it.

- Works with the CEO to identify who else should be a member of the Advisory Board. The strategic plan will identify the capabilities needed for the organisation to execute its strategy. This will clarify the ideal experience and skill set required from other Advisory Board members.

- Identifies and reaches out to prospective members with the CEO, and secures those appropriate.

- Ensures that the Advisory Board achieves its objectives and meets its terms of reference.

- Ensures each meeting is planned, focused on key issues, and executed well.

- Organises the minutes/actions. The Chair will ensure the validity of the minutes taken. As final decisions are the sole responsibility of the CEO, the minutes are typically a list of discussion points, options, prioritisation, and a commitment for the CEO to make decisions after further reflection.

A good Chair makes the meeting work. The Chair ensures the agenda is covered and there is adequate discussion of relevant topics, and then clearly articulates the conclusions drawn from the discussion. They also ensure the CEO derives value from the discussion.

Anecdotal comments from the Lead Your Industry survey effectively highlight the skills needed to be a good Chair. Here's what some survey participants said about what makes a good Chair:

'They're high-calibre and have been in small, medium and large-scale businesses.'

'Clear communication. Good Chairs know when to bring the meeting back on track or let the topic develop further.'

'They lead the meetings, organise them, control the discussions, and encourage discussion where they feel there is more to add.'[11]

---

11 Some quotes were edited for grammatical clarity.

Other Advisory Board members

Start small and grow as needed. I recommend that there be no more than three external Advisory Board members: the Chair and a maximum of two others. I find that beyond that, there are too many voices to be heard, not least as, in addition to the CEO, other executive directors are likely to be in attendance. Equally, the business needs the leadership bandwidth to be able to digest the ideas and if desired implement the ideas that emanate from the meetings.

Desired attributes of all Advisory Board members

Advisory Board members need to have the experience of operating at the board level, not just at the senior executive level. Advisory Board members need to understand their role is one of guidance, mentoring and coaching—it is not directive. That can be a challenge for previous senior executives who made a career based on getting things done and getting others to do things. There is no direct link between a discussion in an Advisory Board meeting and the final action that a CEO chooses to make. Having served on a board is a good demonstration that a potential Advisory Board member has successfully made the transition from executive to board member.

A sense of shared values and an understanding of the organisation's culture are also essential. This not only ensures that meetings run smoothly but also that the advice given will be heard.

Professional integrity—independence

Advisory Board members need to demonstrate their professional integrity. This may mean they sit on other Advisory Boards or are company directors, they have a highly visible industry reputation, or they participate in industry-specific forums or associations. They may also be members of professional bodies such as the Australian Institute of Company Directors (AICD) and may have completed the AICD directors course or be directors of other companies. All of this can be validated via references.

Advisory Board members must be independent, meaning they have no ties to relevant stakeholders that may influence their advice. Of course, they must also have the strength of character to provide the CEO and other board members with frank and fearless advice.

Confidentiality and conflicts of interest

All prospective members must respect the company's confidentiality agreement and commit to transparency when declaring perceived or real conflicts of interest. Specific legal advice should be sought for the correct confidentiality documentation needed for your organisation.

Specific skills

Advisory Board members will also need to have the specific skills that have been identified as necessary in the strategic planning process that will provide the greatest leverage in executing that plan. This means specific domains and best-in-class skills. Examples of specific skills/experience might include international market experience, strategic finance or capital raising expertise, global supply chain management, international marketing, relevant industry compliance, connections to government, deep customer segment knowledge, and technological expertise. These are the specific skills the organisation needs to be able to absorb as it grows.

The Advisory Board member can advise on the best way for the organisation to internalise those skills, in what stages and over what timeframe. This means some Advisory Board members' tenure may have a natural term limit. Once the organisation has achieved the necessary scale and internalised those specific skills, it may be appropriate for that member to move on, perhaps replaced with a board member with more relevant skills for the next growth stage. This is the normal process of renewal that the Chair and CEO will manage, ensuring the continued relevance of the Advisory Board.

'We appointed our Advisory Board to seek fresh input to challenge our thinking, add depth and structure to the review of our business, and prepare the business for my reduced involvement over time.'

CEO SURVEY RESPONDENT

Remuneration

Yes, you should remunerate your Advisory Board members. Now, this may come across as self-serving, as sitting on Advisory Boards and other boards is part of my business, but let me explain. You will certainly be able to find those gracious persons who have succeeded and are keen to give back, which is great at first. However, in my experience, not having a remuneration package means that there is no mutual obligation. After some time, attention starts to waver, and the dynamic changes may materialise in missed board meetings or members not prepping for meetings. To be effective, your Advisory Board members must be vested, that is, committed to your business's success. Hence, there needs to be a true value exchange; they are remunerated for their contribution, and the expense obligates the CEO to ensure they extract value from the meetings. Remunerating your Advisory Board members establishes that structure of mutual obligation and accountability.

I have found that establishing a fee per meeting works well—it directly responds to the workload. That fee must cover the meeting and the cost of being engaged with the organisation between meetings.

Any numbers quoted here would be out of date. Please contact me directly for my perspective on current fees. In some start-up scenarios, Advisory Board members can be paid in shares.

How to find the right Advisory Board members

Many CEOs interested in establishing an Advisory Board don't take the first step because they are unsure how to find the right members. Once the purpose and objectives of the Advisory Board have been set and the skills and expertise required are identified from the strategic review, the prospective members' profile becomes clear. Then, it is a case of securing the Chair, who will assist in selecting additional board members.

This is a hiring process, so you must apply the same due diligence as you do when hiring a new senior team member.

The Advisory Board needs to be independent and able to offer frank and fearless advice. Hence, appointing friends or family, even if they may have the appropriate skills, is not recommended. Remember, all things change, and it is generally better to retain your family and friends than to lose them because, at some point, they had to be fired from your Advisory Board.

Advisory Board questionnaire

The following will help you determine the specific experience and skill sets needed from your Advisory Board members.

Rate the importance out of 5 (= must have) of these skills for your Advisory Board members	Rating 1–5
1 Specific industry expertise and connections	
2 Connections—industry-specific—or customer, supplier, professional service providers, or government	
3 Experience scaling a business / driving successful transformation	
4 People management expertise	
5 Strategic financial management (CFO) / capital raising / M&A	
6 Experience building international markets	
7 Technical expertise (product-service or end-user related)	
8 Marketing expertise	
9 Expertise in operational excellence	
10 Innovation expertise	
11 Global supply chain management	
12 Technology—systems—AI	
13 Other	

Here's how to identify your ideal Chair:

1 Narrow down one or two candidates who would be an ideal Chair. They may have a high profile in your industry or are renowned as industry experts in a particular domain of expertise.

2 Explore your first- and second-level connections (including your leadership team and their connections) for introductions to those ideal people.

3 Engage your professional network, i.e. accountant, lawyer and business advisers (Lead Your Industry), for specific recommendations.

4 Reach out to specific candidates and explore the opportunity of a relationship; people are flattered to be asked and are willing to engage. Even those who may not be interested will normally make recommendations.

In my experience, the above process will generate several fit-for-purpose candidates. The next step is to start engaging and explore if there is also an appetite and a cultural fit.

On the rare occasion that this process has not generated sufficient candidates, engaging with organisations like the AICD may be appropriate. The AICD provides a platform to advertise your requirements to its 40,000+ members.

The Advisory Board Centre is also a commercial organisation that offers training courses for advisers seeking to join Advisory Boards and may also be a source of prospects.

Once you've selected from the candidate pool, the next steps are:

- Complete interviews, follow up references and decide— make the offer, clarify remuneration and share the Charter.

- Ensure all legal documentation, e.g., confidentiality and appointment letter, are duly executed.

- Once appointed, all relevant historical information should be shared, including performance history, strategic plans, and recent successes and failures. It is important that the new member has as complete a picture of the business as possible and understands the CEO's ambition and risk appetite.

Measures of success

Having an Advisory Board requires a commitment in time (for prep and attending meetings) and funds. Like all commercial arrangements, it needs to deliver a return. That value return can only be determined by the CEO.

There are two evaluations that should be considered annually.

1   Is the Advisory Board providing value to the CEO?

2   Are the individual members of the Advisory Board making a valued contribution?

Is the Advisory Board providing value to the CEO?

In regard to the first question, the CEO evaluates performance by asking him or herself the following questions:

- Is my time well spent in Advisory Board meetings? Would I rather be in those meetings, or is my time better spent elsewhere?

- Is the Advisory Board the best it can be? If you would rate it less than eight out of ten, what would need to change for the rating to be higher?

Of course, these questions, which are primarily subjective, need to be explored with the Chair, along with a more objective assessment of whether the Advisory Board achieved its remit.

Each year, the Advisory Board should establish core topics for review. These can be in terms of a focus on specific issues such as fast-tracking a growth strategy, upskilling the leadership team in a particular area, or analysing operational performance. At the end of the year, the CEO and

Chair can determine the degree to which core objectives were addressed. In addition, the Advisory Board needs to have the flexibility to address issues with the CEO and the business as they arise.

Are Advisory Board members each making a valued contribution?

In response to the second evaluation question, the CEO and the Chair must ask the following:

- Has the individual contributed to the overall effectiveness of the Advisory Board meetings?

- Has the individual contributed through applying the specific commercial or technical expertise for which they were appointed for the benefit of the CEO and organisation?

With the answers to these key questions, if warranted, the Chair or the CEO will adjust the meeting structure, frequency and duration of meetings or decide to change the members. Again, the CEO retains control!

CASE STUDY
MAKINEX PTY LTD

Makinex Pty Ltd is a privately owned company at the forefront of innovation, designing and manufacturing tools and power sources for construction jobsites. Since its foundation in 2004, the business has grown substantially, winning design and industry awards, establishing distributors in multiple countries and opening a subsidiary in the USA. Its most recent innovation is the development of a range of industry-leading Renewable Power solutions for construction sites.

Founder and CEO Rory Kennard appointed an Advisory Board back in 2012. Over the years, a number of members joined who had the expertise the organisation needed for its next stage of growth and, equally, members have left the Advisory Board as its leadership has matured.

The Advisory Board has been a constant in stress-testing the strategic initiatives developed by the leadership.

The following is an extract from an article that first appeared in the AICD magazine, *Company Director*, in June 2019.[12]

Makinex co-founder and CEO (Rory) Kennard is a mechanical engineer who began designing and selling construction products under his industrial and architectural design business, Kennovations, after graduating from university. He heads up a four-person research and development department, which builds its prototypes in a Sydney factory and manufactures mostly (60 per cent) in Sydney, but also in China, Spain and the US.

---

12   https://www.aicd.com.au/corporate-governance-sectors/global/challenges/makinex.html

Six years ago, Makinex took on business coach Anthony Moss GAICD, who now chairs the Advisory Board. Moss facilitated the creation of a 10-year plan—broken into three and four-year chunks, with goals to be reviewed regularly and reset as needed. Its initial goal—to have a range of 20 world-first products in 20 countries within 10 years, and a $40m turnover.

The company's new goal is to create 20 product ranges, each with a turnover of $5m: 'We want a $100m business.'

In April 2023, with the business having increased in size and complexity and faced with significant growth opportunities, CEO Kennard desired a more formal structure. He dissolved the Advisory Board and appointed a Governance Board with non-executive directors.

The Advisory Board has contributed to the directors' thinking over many years. Still, as the business was now more sophisticated in scale and leadership talent, the Advisory Board was retired as it had served its purpose.

Advisory Board evaluation table

The following is a simple framework example for evaluating your Advisory Board.

CEO and Chair responses

	Rating 1-10	What needs to be true to score 10?
THE ADVISORY BOARD GENERALLY		
CEO: Is my time well spent in the AB meetings?	8	E.g. Clearer conclusions from the meetings.
Is the AB the best that it could be?	7	E.g. We need an additional member with xx skills. One member is retiring.
Overall score for the Advisory Board	7.5	E.g. A new member is needed.
INDIVIDUAL BOARD MEMBERS		
Chair		
Contribution to meetings	9	
Application of specific commercial and or / technical skills	8	
Overall rating	8.5	
BOARD MEMBER 1		
Contribution to meetings	9	
Application of specific commercial and or / technical skills	8	
Overall rating	8.5	
BOARD MEMBER 2		
Contribution to meetings	6	E.g. Can go off on a tangent, creating a distraction.
Application of specific commercial and or / technical skills	8	
Overall rating	7	
ACTIONS		
Chair to coach board member 2		
Chair to secure new board members with expertise in...		

Retiring an Advisory Board member

Members of an Advisory Board are appointed at the CEO's pleasure. This means the CEO determines the length of time a particular member sits on an Advisory Board. That said, an Advisory Board takes some time to reach its peak effectiveness and should be given at least twelve months to perform. At some point, removing a sitting Advisory Board member may become necessary. It could be that the business has evolved, and the skills an Advisory Board member originally brought to the table are now embedded in the organisation. It could also be due to a lack of cultural fit, poor performance or, worse, a breach of the terms of engagement.

The terms of engagement when appointing an Advisory Board member also outline how the member's tenure ends.

If the CEO and/or the Chair believe a board member is no longer adding value to the meetings, the Chair should advise the board member accordingly and cease the arrangement in accordance with the agreed terms.

In short, Advisory Board members are there at the will of the CEO—this is one of the core distinctions from a Governance Board and gives the CEO confidence that they have complete flexibility to craft an Advisory Board that is fit for purpose and have the freedom to make changes when appropriate.

Retiring an Advisory Board

As the business evolves and becomes more complex, with talented leaders, the CEO may decide that the Advisory Board is no longer needed. This is not uncommon and validates the fit-for-purpose nature of an Advisory Board, that is, it is valuable when established and flexible enough to transform as the business grows and needs change. Finally, it can be retired at will when the organisation has built the necessary capability in-house or where the governance requirement has changed.

QUESTIONS FOR REFLECTION

1   Are you prepared to listen to alternative perspectives that might challenge your own?

2   Are you prepared to have someone else chair the Advisory Board meetings?

3   Are you prepared to meet for two or three hours every month, bi-monthly or quarterly?

4   Would an Advisory Board enable you to converse better with fellow shareholders/directors?

5   Will the Advisory Board be able to manage the often-conflicting voices of your family dynamic?

6   What is the opportunity cost of not changing now?

7   Who would be the ideal person to chair your Advisory Board?

8   Who would be the next best ideal person to be Chair?

9   Who do you know that has a relationship to those ideal candidates?

10 Who within your professional network—accountants, lawyers, business advisers, industry or professional association members—will likely have appropriate connections?

Conclusion

AS I SAID in Chapter 1, appointing an Advisory Board is not for the faint-hearted. CEOs who appoint an Advisory Board must be comfortable hearing alternative opinions. Contrarian views and challenging perspectives are baked into the structure of an Advisory Board.

An Advisory Board provides a safe and confidential environment where discussions are held, and issues are explored that help the CEO develop and make better business decisions. With the full benefits outlined in Chapter 3, the Advisory Board can become integral to the CEO's development—such that it runs for a long time.

Pressure and the role of the CEO go hand-in-hand. The title infers that the bearer innately has the skills to get the job done, inspire their team, and have all the right answers or approaches for all stakeholders. In reality, few people are so great. There may be capabilities that they excel at and others that might be best described as 'in development'. Some CEOs prefer to be solely responsible for their destiny; taking the hard knocks and learning from them. That is certainly an option, but in my experience, that decision tends to lead to very bumpy outcomes for the CEO, their organisation and their people.

I invite you to see an alternative, to springboard your and your team's learning by surrounding yourself with the Sherpas who have already climbed the mountain you have set your sights on. They know the dangerous sections, the easier route, and the slower and faster routes.

Using an Advisory Board as a guide, organisations improve, make better decisions, achieve their objectives more swiftly, think differently about their business, and often develop new opportunities. Along the way, the CEO and leadership team develop their skills and capabilities most appropriately, with confidence that they are making the right decisions for them. When the leadership team builds capability, they build capability for the business. That leads to resilience, better performance, faster growth, more profitability, and less stress for the CEO.

An Advisory Board is not a magic bullet; it is not a panacea for a misguided strategy or for a rapidly disappearing market. However, the right Advisory Board will enable you to see potential flaws in your response to market conditions or open your eyes to new opportunities. It will help you respond differently, considering all options in relation to your purpose and business appetite. An objective perspective will enable you to make the right decisions for your business.

In my experience, CEOs interested in an Advisory Board seek to have a much bigger impact on their industry, their end-user and the people who work in their organisations. They see an Advisory Board as a game changer for better business, one that, in their chosen way, enables them to lead their industry.

FINAL QUESTIONS FOR REFLECTION

1   Do you have a qualified, high-performing leadership team?

2   Is your growth strategy clear to all your people?

3   What does success look like for you personally?

4   What do you not know that would make the execution of your strategy much easier, quicker and more effective? (Or make your strategy better.)

5   How stressed is your organisation?

6   How do you know when your mindset is right when you are on or off your game?

Acknowledgements

I WANT TO thank all the people who have contributed to my journey of understanding business. To those who supported and contributed to my early development: Jon Sulkin, Export Director at Daler-Rowney, Jim Daler, Group Managing Director of Daler-Rowney, and my partners from Incite Management Group who supported my start in the consulting industry, particularly Blair Saddington, who is a constant, trusted colleague.

I would like to thank the many clients I have worked with over the years and from whom I have learned so much. Special thanks to Rory Kennard, CEO of Makinex, Bill Morrison, co-founder of the Conybeare Morrison Group, Naomi and Anthony Green, co-founders of Tiger Tribe, and of course the members of the peer-to-peer group I chair, the CEO Advisory Board.

The above have graciously allowed me the opportunity to contribute to the growth of their businesses. They are determined, passionate, entrepreneurial, and great at what they do but also wise enough to be open and vulnerable and surround themselves with people who think differently and challenge their perspective. I would like to thank Matt

Church and his Thought Leaders Business School, which gave me a framework that enabled me to clarify my thinking and an 'accountability' support network that brought this book to fruition. In addition, my 'brand manager' and good friend Wayne Lazarides has been an invaluable sounding board to sharpen my thinking and communication strategy.

Finally, a huge thank you to my Business Manager, Jenny Thomson, who has supported my business and my foibles for many years.

Let's Connect and Grow Your Business

Join the CEO Advisory Board

IF YOU ARE unsure whether establishing an Advisory Board for your business is the right thing to do but know that you need to surround yourself with peers and experts who think differently, there are alternatives. I created the CEO Advisory Board for this reason.

The CEO Advisory Board is a group of CEOs from non-competing industries who meet on a monthly basis to discuss, share, learn and develop. Working as the optimum model of an Advisory Board, all members learn from each other's experience and expertise as well as guest subject matter experts.

Within the parameters of a code of conduct and a mutual confidentiality agreement, the CEO Advisory Board is a safe and supportive space to share the challenges and opportunities that keep CEOs awake at night.

That said, three key differences exist between this model and establishing your own Advisory Board.

1   You do not get to choose your peers in the group.

2   As this is a group-learning model, there is inevitably limited time to discuss your issues. The others in the group also need time to explore their issues.

3   The investment in the CEO Advisory Board is considerably less than the cost of establishing your own Advisory Board.

Please reach out if you would like to explore joining the CEO Advisory Board.

Contact me at anthonym@leadyourindustry.com.

Testimonials from members of the CEO Advisory Board

'Being part of a CEO peer group offered me a unique array of benefits that transcend ordinary connections. Beyond family and friends, this group has provided deep, meaningful connections rooted in shared experiences and mutual understanding. It has served as an invaluable sounding board where ideas are honed and refined through collective wisdom and diverse perspectives.

One of the greatest assets is accountability: we challenge each other to navigate difficult conversations with honesty and respect. Moreover, the safe and mature environment allows for the exploration of differing viewpoints on pressing issues. The CEO Advisory group is a cornerstone for leadership development with a healthy mix of ridiculous health challenges and loads of humour.'

ERICA WESTBURY, Managing Director, Norwest Recruitment, www.norwestrecruitment.com.au

'We so often surround ourselves with like-minded people. An Advisory Board is the perfect chance to hear from people who possess different biases and, therefore, may give a different perspective on a problem or strategy. Thinking outside the square is so often what has produced quantum leaps in history. I have found the CEO Advisory Board is a big step in that direction.'

STEVEN PATTERSON, Managing Director, Derivan Pty Ltd, www.derivan.com.au

'As a sole shareholder and director, the CEO Advisory Board is where I go to share my ideas, concepts, try new things out, ask questions I can't anywhere else, learn and be inspired.

It is a peer group like no other, and I rely on it to sustain my CEO mindset, find out about the cutting-edge issues in business, reset priorities, and think about the future of my firm. It's been a great commercial support and a source of friendship and camaraderie."

FELICITY ZADRO, BA, MA, GAICD, Founder and CEO, ZADRO, www.zadroagency.com.au

Step One
The Right Strategy

IN THIS BOOK, I mention that your strategic plan unveils the skills and experience necessary for joining your Advisory Board; hence, the prospects' profile to join is obvious. If your strategic plan is not crystal clear or you don't have one, establishing your strategic plan is step one.

The most challenging aspect of leading a business is navigating the inherently imperfect world of allocating limited resources while anticipating or responding to external threats and opportunities.

The Right Strategy™ liberates the organisation from being merely opportunistic to being able to evaluate and take advantage of the right opportunities. Using a sailing analogy, it's the difference between merely following the direction of the wind blowing in any direction and charting a course to arrive at a specific destination.

Customer perceptions of value are changing rapidly; what was a groundbreaking innovation yesterday is the new norm today. New business models are upending industries; it's far easier for agile start-ups to commence with an innovative business model than for established mid-size businesses to shift gears. The pull of 'business as usual' is powerful.

The Right Strategy for your organisation provides direction, the north star you seek, and the framework for navigating the tension between current commercial requirements and long-term strategic goals.

The subject of my next book is how to develop The Right Strategy, which exists at the intersection of your Purpose, Potential and Appetite.

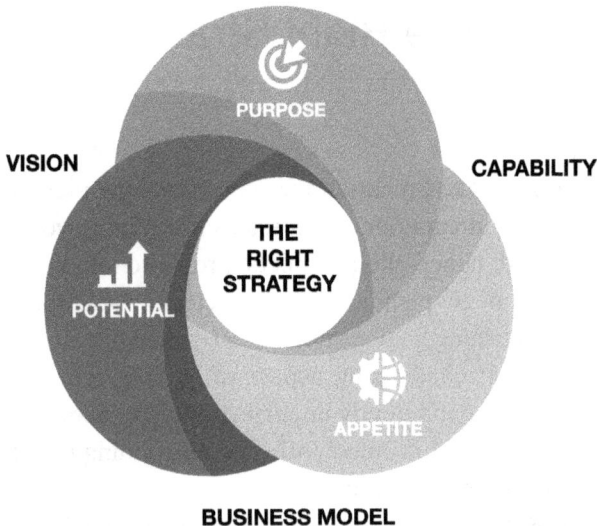

PURPOSE

VISION

CAPABILITY

THE RIGHT STRATEGY

POTENTIAL

APPETITE

BUSINESS MODEL

FIGURE 6 The Right Strategy

The process of choosing The Right Strategy is transformative, resulting in outcomes that typically include:

- perspective and new insight about the potential of your business

- an inspired vision that articulates the impact your business wishes to make and motivates your stakeholders

- a clear pathway to 'winning'

- an updated or new business model

- an energised leadership team focused on measuring and managing the right things

- clarity about the skills and resources you need to implement your strategic plan

Need help developing The Right Strategy for your organisation? Reach out to me at anthonym@leadyourindustry.com.

Engaging with Anthony Moss and Lead Your Industry

My consulting practice, Lead Your Industry Pty Ltd (www.leadyourindustry.com), is focused on unleashing the potential of private companies. I have seen both great success and the impact of failure, and my mission is to assist CEOs in building great businesses for the benefit of their people, the community and, of course, sustainable profit.

I have written this book based on my experience as a CEO, executive director, non-executive director/chair, and chair of several Advisory Boards. I believe passionately in the structure of an Advisory Board as a springboard for success that builds sustainable foundations for long-term value creation. An organisation is not required to have an Advisory Board. Still, in my experience, at the right stage of development, those CEOs who choose this route attest to the benefit to their businesses.

I offer a range of relevant services, including:

- Board / leadership strategy facilitation

- Advisory Board and Governance Board roles

- The CEO Advisory Board (peer-to-peer Advisory Board, Sydney based)

Please contact me via the website or directly via email at anthonym@leadyourindustry.com for a complimentary discussion about how an Advisory Board or a strategy refresh may be the game changer your organisation needs.

Appendix
Advisory Board Questionnaire

THIS QUESTIONNAIRE was sent to CEOs with Advisory Boards in September 2020 and garnered submissions from thirty-two respondents.

1 How long has your Advisory Board been in existence?

2 What catalyst made you decide to appoint an Advisory Board?

3 On a scale of one to ten, how likely are you to recommend establishing an Advisory Board for CEOs of private companies? (One being the lowest and ten being the highest.) Can you explain why you gave that score?

4 On a scale of one to ten, how would you rate the value of your Advisory Board? (One being the lowest and ten being the highest.) Can you explain why you gave that score?

5 How could the effectiveness of your Advisory Board be improved?

6 Please rate the specific elements of value of your Advisory Board by rating the criteria below, one being the lowest rating (disagree) and five being the highest rating (agree):

- It holds me accountable

- There is new/different thinking from our Advisory Board

- Our Advisory Board brings new/different skills

- Our Advisory Board is an important element in our approach to Corporate Governance

- Our Advisory Board shares access to their networks (customers, suppliers, government)

- Our Advisory Board meetings are safe and confidential

- Our Advisory Board enables us to envision potential for the business we had not previously thought of

- Our Advisory Board provides mentoring for the CEO

- We make better decisions because of the Advisory Board

- Our strategic planning is more robust because of our Advisory Board

7 What would you like to change about your Advisory Board?

8 Describe the impact your Advisory Board has had on you, your fellow directors and the business.

9 Please describe the attributes necessary to be a good Advisory Board member.

10 Please describe the attributes of a good Advisory Board Chair.

11 To be effective, please describe how the CEO needs to approach engaging with an Advisory Board.

12 What can go wrong when appointing an Advisory Board?

13 Would you be prepared to be interviewed about the performance of your Advisory Board?